Acts

AWAKENING TO GOD

in Everyday Life

A BIBLE STUDY BY

MELISSA SPOELSTRA

Abingdon Women| Nashville

Acts:
Awakening to God in Everyday Life
Leader Guide

ISBN 978-1-5018-7822-0

21 22 23 24 25 26 27 28 29 30—10 9 8 7 6 5 4 3 2 1
MANUFACTURED IN THE UNITED STATES OF AMERICA

Contents

About the Author

Melissa Spoelstra is a popular women's conference speaker (including the Aspire Tour), Bible teacher, and author who is madly in love with Jesus and passionate about studying God's Word and helping women of all ages to seek Christ and know Him more intimately through serious Bible study. Having a degree in Bible theology, she enjoys teaching God's Word to the body of Christ and traveling to diverse groups and churches across the nation and also to Nairobi, Kenya, for a women's prayer conference. Melissa is the author of the Bible studies *The Names of God: His Character Revealed*, *Romans: Good News That Changes Everything*, *Elijah: Spiritual Stamina in Every Season*, *Numbers: Learning Contentment in a Culture of More*, *First Corinthians: Living Love When We Disagree*, *Joseph: The Journey to Forgiveness*, and *Jeremiah: Daring to Hope in an Unstable World*, and the books *Dare to Hope: Living Intentionally in an Unstable World*, *Total Family Makeover: 8 Practical Steps to Making Disciples at Home*, and *Total Christmas Makeover: 31 Devotions to Celebrate with Purpose*. She is a regular contributor to the Proverbs 31 First Five App and the Girlfriends in God online daily devotional. She has published articles in *ParentLife*, *Women's Spectrum*, and *Just Between Us* and writes her own regular blog in which she shares her musings about what God is teaching her on any given day. Melissa lives in Pickerington, Ohio, with her pastor husband, Sean, and their four kids: Zach, Abby, Sara, and Rachel.

Follow Melissa:

- 🐦 @MelSpoelstra
- 📷 @Daring2Hope
- 📘 @Author MelissaSpoelstra

Her blog MelissaSpoelstra.com
(check here also for event dates and booking information)

Introduction to this Study

The word *awakening* makes me think of mornings, and I've never been accused of being a morning person. My alarm jolts me awake on weekdays, and immediately the mental bargaining begins as I consider reasons to hit snooze. Even though I love sleep, awakening is essential to living life. When I wake up, I experience sights and sounds that I wasn't conscious of while asleep. I have full awareness of myself and my surroundings.

Just as we awaken physically each day, so we must awaken spiritually in our everyday lives. Each day we need to open our spiritual eyes and ears to experience the power and presence of God with a fresh perspective. As you lead your group for this study of the Book of Acts, I pray that women will discover a spiritual awareness for their own lives as we witness God's Spirit birth and grow the early church by awakening them to His power, message, freedom, grace, mission, and direction.

About the Participant Workbook

Before the first session, you will want to distribute copies of the participant workbook to the members of your group. Be sure to communicate that they are to complete the first week of readings *before* your Week 1 session. (If you plan to have an Introductory Session, they will begin the homework after that.) Each week, five readings or lessons will combine study of Scripture with personal reflection and application (boldface type indicates write-in-the-book questions and activities). Each lesson ends with a "Talk with God" prayer suggestion.

On average, you will need about twenty to thirty minutes for each lesson. Completing these readings each week will prepare the women for the discussion and activities of the group session.

About This Leader Guide

As you gather each week with the members of your group, you will have the opportunity to watch a video, discuss and respond to what you're learning, and pray together. You will need access to a television and a DVD player with working remotes (or stream through the AmplifyMedia.com subscription. See page 208 of the participant workbook.)

Creating a warm and inviting atmosphere will make the women feel welcome. Although optional, you might consider providing snacks for your first meeting and inviting group members to rotate in bringing refreshments each week.

This leader guide and the video will be your primary tools for leading your group on this journey through Acts. Whether you choose to follow this guide step by step, modify its contents to meet your group's needs and preferences, or simply peruse it to find a few helpful tips, questions, and ideas, in these pages you will find some valuable tools for creating a successful group experience.

Getting Started: This is a list of strategies, options, and introductory information that will help you ensure good organization and communication. You will want to review this material and share relevant information with group members prior to your group session for Week 1, either via e-mail or in an introductory session. Or you might consider adding fifteen to thirty minutes to your first session for reviewing some of these important housekeeping details. Whichever option you choose, be sure that group members have the opportunity to purchase books and complete Week 1 before your session for Week 1.

Tips for Tackling Five Common Challenges: This section includes ideas for addressing recurring issues that come up when leading a group. Every leader knows that some group dynamics can be difficult to tackle. What will you do when one person dominates the discussion or cuts off another person who is speaking? All eyes will be on you to see how you will intervene or ignore these situations. Be sure to check out these five common challenges and ideas to help when you encounter them.

Basic Leader Helps: This list of basic leader tips will help you prepare for and lead each group session.

Session Outlines: This guide contains six adaptable outlines to help guide your group time each week. Each begins with a "Leader Prep" section to assist with preparation.

This study is designed for six weeks, with an optional introductory session. Or, if desired, you may choose to extend the study to eight or twelve weeks (see the options included in "Getting Started"). Each of the session outlines in this book may be used for a 60-minute, 90-minute, or 120-minute session. The following formats are offered as templates that you may modify for your group:

60-Minute Format

Welcome/Fellowship (2 minutes)

All Play (3 minutes)

Prayer and Video (25–30 minutes)

Group Discussion (20 minutes)

Prayer Requests (5 minutes)

90-Minute Format

Welcome/Fellowship (5–10 minutes)

All Play (5 minutes)

Prayer and Video (25–30 minutes)

Group Discussion (25 minutes)

Optional Group Activity (5–10 minutes)

Prayer Requests (10 minutes)

120-Minute Format

Welcome/Fellowship (10–15 minutes)

All Play (5–10 minutes)

Prayer and Video (25–30 minutes)

Group Discussion (30–35 minutes)

Optional Group Activity (10 minutes)
Prayer Requests (15–20 minutes)

As you can see, the basic elements remain the same in each format: a welcome/ fellowship time, an "All Play" icebreaker question that everyone can answer, a video segment, group discussion, and prayer time. The 90-minute and 120-minute options offer longer times for fellowship, discussion, and prayer plus an optional group activity. If you choose not to do the group activity, you may add that time to another element of the session, such as group discussion or prayer. (See "Getting Started" for notes about including food, planning for childcare, and other important organizational details.)

If you are either new to leading Bible studies or would like to have a framework to follow, or both, the session outlines will guide you. I have provided more discussion questions than you may have time to include. Before the session, choose the questions you want to cover and put a check mark beside them. Page references are provided for those questions that relate to questions or activities in the participant workbook. For these questions, invite group members to turn in their participant workbooks to the pages indicated.

If you are a seasoned group leader looking only for a few good questions or ideas, I encourage you to take what you want and leave the rest. After all, you know your group better than I do! Ask God to show you what areas to focus on from each week's homework and use my discussion outline as a template you can revise.

Of course, the Holy Spirit knows the content of this study (His Word) and the women in your group better than anyone else, so above all, I encourage you to lead this study under the Holy Spirit's direction, allowing yourself the freedom to make any changes or adaptations that are helpful or desirable.

I'm so excited that God has called you to lead a group of ladies through a study of the names of God. Know that I am praying for you and believing God for the work He will do through your leadership. Now, let's get started!

Melissa

Getting Started

Before your study begins, be sure to review the following introductory information that will help you ensure good organization and communication. I encourage you to share relevant information such as the dates, times, and location for group meetings; when/where/how to purchase books; details regarding childcare and food; expectations and ground rules; and an overview of the study to group members. This can be covered during an introductory session or via e-mail before your session for Week 1.

1. Determine the length of your study. The basic study is designed for six weeks (plus an optional introductory session), but you also can plan for an eight- or twelve-week study.

    - *For a six-week study*—plus an additional (optional) introductory session if desired—use the session guides in this book and the video segments (DVD or streaming files). Be sure to distribute books during the introductory session (if you are having one) or prior to your group session for Week 1.

    - *For an eight-week study*, add both an introductory session and a closing celebration. In the introductory session, watch the introductory video message and spend time getting to know one another, presenting basic housekeeping information, and praying together (use the guide on pages 16–17). For a closing celebration, discuss what you have learned together in a special gathering that includes refreshments or perhaps a brunch, luncheon, or supper. A closing celebration provides an excellent opportunity for ongoing groups to invite friends and reach out to others who might be interested in joining the group for a future study.

- To allow more time for completing homework, extend the study to twelve weeks. This is especially helpful for groups with mothers of young children or women carrying a heavy work or ministry schedule. With this option, women have two weeks in which to complete each week of homework in the participant workbook. In your group sessions, watch and discuss the video the first week; then review and discuss homework the next week. Some women find they are better able to complete assignments and digest what they are learning this way.

2. Determine the length of each group session (60, 90, or 120 minutes). See the format templates outlined on pages 7–8.

3. Decide ahead of time if you/your church will purchase participant workbooks that group members can buy in advance during an introductory session or in advance of your first session, or if group members will buy their own books individually. If you expect each member to buy her own book, e-mail group members purchasing information (be sure to note the cost, including tax and shipping if applicable). Consider including online links as well. Be sure to allow enough time for participants to purchase books and complete the readings for Week 1 prior to your group session for Week 1.

4. Create a group roster that includes each group member's name, e-mail address, mailing address, and primary phone number. (Collect this information through registration, e-mail, or an introductory session.) Distribute copies of the roster to group members prior to or during your first session. A group roster enables group members to stay connected and contact one another freely as needed, such as when taking a meal or sending a card to someone who is sick, who has missed several group sessions, or who has had a baby or is experiencing another significant life event. Group members may want to meet for coffee or lunch to follow up on things shared in the study as well. As women cry and laugh and share life together in a Bible study, their lives will be intertwined, even if for a short time.

5. Make decisions about childcare and food and communicate this information to group members in advance. Will childcare be offered, and will there be a cost associated with it? Will refreshments be served at your gatherings?

(*Note*: If your group is meeting for 60 minutes, you will not have time for a formal fellowship time with refreshments. You might consider having refreshments set up early and inviting women to come a few minutes before the session officially begins.) If you choose to have food, the introductory meeting is a good time to pass around a sign-up sheet. In the Bible study group I lead, we like to eat, so we have three women sign up to bring food for each meeting. One brings fruit, another brings bread or muffins, and another brings an egg dish. Your group may want to keep it simple; just be mindful of food allergies and provide choices.

6. Let group members know what to expect. Those who have never participated in a women's Bible study group may be intimidated, scared, or unsure of what to expect. Friends have told me that when they first came to Bible study, they were concerned they would be called on to pray out loud or expected to know everything in the Bible. Ease group members' concerns up front. Reassure the women that they will not be put on the spot and that they may choose to share as they are comfortable. Encourage participation while fostering a safe environment. Laying a few basic ground rules such as these can help you achieve this kind of setting:

   - *Confidentiality*. Communicate that anything shared in the group is not to be repeated outside of those present in the study. Women need to feel safe to be vulnerable and authentic.

   - *Sensitivity*. Talk about courtesy, which includes practices such as refraining from interrupting, monopolizing, or trying to "fix" shared problems. Women want to be heard, not told what to do, when they share an issue in their lives. If they have advice to share with an individual, ask them to speak with the person privately after the study. When studying God's Word, some differences of opinion are bound to arise regarding either interpretation and application, or both. This is a good place to sharpen one another and respectfully disagree so that you may grow and understand different viewpoints. Remind the women that it's OK to question and see things differently; however, they must be kind and sensitive to the feelings of others.

- *Purpose.* The primary reason you are taking time out of your busy schedules to meet together is to study the Bible. Though your group will pray for, serve, and support one another, your primary focus is to study the Bible. You learn in community from one another as you draw near to God through His Word. Though you may want to plan a service or social activity during the course of your study, these times should be secondary to your study time together. If group members express a desire for the group to do more outreach, service, or socials, gently remind them of the primary reason you gather.

7. Before the study begins, provide a short preview of the study's content, summarizing highlights in an e-mail or introductory session. You might whet the appetite for what is to come by sharing (or reading) parts of the introduction from the participant workbook. Consider sharing a personal story that relates to the study's theme. As Christ-followers, we need a fresh encounter with God. On many occasions I need to be reminded of God's vast love in order to be better equipped to handle daily battles and share God's love with one another. As I go from errand to errand, I look at the gas gauge in my car and see the needle pointing toward E for empty, yet I keep driving from place to place without stopping to fill the tank with much-needed new fuel. Think of times you have done the same. What made you drive on? Now think of the times you stopped to refuel your tank. How did it feel to stop and refuel your tank with much-needed fresh fuel? Let's pray our study together will empower us to seek and find that fresh encounter with God.

8. If you are having an introductory session, show the introductory video and open the floor for women to share in response to the questions on page 24.

9. *Be sure to communicate to participants that they are to complete Week 1 in the participant workbook prior to your group session for Week 1.* Review the options for study found in the introduction to the participant workbook and encourage participants to choose the options they plan to complete and then share this information with someone in the group for accountability.

Tips for Tackling Five Common Challenges

Challenge #1: Preparation

Do you know that feeling when Bible study is in two days and you haven't even finished the homework, much less prepared for the group session? We've all been there. When I'm unprepared, I can sense the difference in how I teach Sunday school, lead VBS, or facilitate discussion in my women's Bible study group. I'm hurried, scattered, and less confident when I haven't dedicated the proper time for preparation. It doesn't take hours, but it does take commitment.

I check myself with a little acronym when I prepare to lead: S-S-S. Many years ago, I was asked to lead a segment on teacher training for a group of VBS leaders. I remember asking the Lord, "What are the most important things to remember when we handle your Word to teach?" As I sat listening, He gave me this process of S-S-S that has stuck with me through the years. It looks like this:

S — **Savior.** Know your Savior. We must spend time talking, listening, and staying closely connected with Jesus in order to lead well. As we intentionally keep our walk with Him close and vibrant, we can then hear His voice about how to structure our lesson, what questions to ask, and which verses in His Word to focus on.

S — **Story.** Know your story. Though God has been gracious to me when I have winged it, I feel the most freedom with God's truth when I have prepared thoroughly. Try not to cram in multiple days of homework at one time. Let it sink into your soul by reading curiously and slowly. Go back to areas that especially strike you and allow God to use His Word in your heart and mind so that you can teach with authenticity. Women can tell when you are flying by the seat of your pants.

S — **Students.** Know your students. Who are these women God has given you to shepherd? Are they struggling with finances, relationships, or body image issues? Are they mature Christ-followers who need to be challenged to go deeper in their study of God's Word, or are they seekers who need extra explanation about where the books of the Bible are located? Most likely, you will be teaching to a wide range of backgrounds as well as emotional and spiritual maturity levels, and you will need God's wisdom and guidance to inspire them.

Challenge #2: Group Dynamics

Have you experienced that uncomfortable feeling when you ask a discussion question and a long silence settles over the group? With your eyes begging someone to break the ice, you wonder if you should let the question linger or jump in with your own answer. Other problems with group dynamics surface when Silent Suzy never contributes to the conversation because Talking Tammy answers every question. What does a good leader do in these situations? While every group has a unique vibe, I have found these general concepts very helpful in facilitating discussion:

First of all, a good leader asks questions. Jesus was our greatest example. He definitely taught spiritual truths, but one of His most effective methods was asking questions. Proverbs 20:5 says, "Though good advice lies deep within the heart, / a person with understanding will draw it out." As leaders, we must be intentional askers and listeners. I try to gauge myself throughout the discussion by reflecting often on this simple question: "Am I doing all the talking?" When I find I am hearing my own voice too much, I make a point to ask and listen more. Even if waiting means a little silence hangs in the air, eventually someone will pipe up and share. Women learn from one another's insights and experiences; we rob them of others' wisdom when we monopolize as leaders.

Now, what about Chatty Chelsy? She not only answers every question but also makes a comment after each woman shares something (often relating to one of her own experiences). Try one of these transitional statements:

- "Thanks, Chelsy, let's see if someone else has some insight as well."
- "Let's hear from someone who hasn't shared yet today."
- "Is there anyone who hasn't talked much today who would be willing to answer this question?"

The hope is Chatty Chelsy will realize that she has had a lot of floor time.

Sometimes Chatty Chelsy also struggles to "land the plane." She can't find a stopping place in her story. Help her out by jumping in when she takes a breath and make a summary statement for her. For example, "I hear you saying that you can relate to the difficulty of hearing God during a waiting season. Has anyone else experienced this struggle with feeling God's power in His time instead of what you expected?" Occasionally, I have had to take someone aside in a loving way and address her amount of talking. Pray hard and be gentle, but address the issue. As a leader, you must keep in mind the good of the group as a whole.

I once had several ladies leave the group because they were so frustrated by the continual barrage of talking by one woman in particular. Some of her many comments were insensitive and offensive to others in the room. I don't like confrontation, so I didn't want to address it. However, God grew me as a leader to speak loving truth, even when it hurts, for the benefit of those we are called to shepherd.

Sometimes even more challenging than Chatty Chelsy is Silent Suzy. We must walk a fine line as leaders, not putting on the spot those women who are uncomfortable talking in front of others. I have scared women away by being too direct. So how do we get Silent Suzy to talk without singling her out? Here are some ideas:

- If she is new to the study, don't push her at all during the first few sessions. Let her feel safe and get comfortable. Never call on her to pray out loud or single her out with a pointed question. I once said, "I want to know what Suzy thinks about this." All eyes turned on her, and I'll never forget the tears welling in the corners of her eyes as she said she wasn't comfortable being called on. She didn't come back to the group after that incident. I learned a valuable lesson from Silent Suzy—don't push!

- Listen with recall as she answers the All Play question that everyone is asked to answer. Watch for an opportunity to talk about something she has shared by asking a follow-up question that doesn't pry.
- Take her out for coffee and get to know her. With time, she might warm up and begin to contribute to the discussion. Through a deepened relationship, you'll get a better read on whether you should encourage her to talk.

Challenge #3: Prayer Requests

How often do we run out of time when sharing prayer requests, leaving us no time to actually pray? How do you handle those women who aren't comfortable praying out loud? What if your group has fifteen to thirty women, and just listening to everyone's prayer request takes half an hour?

It's so important to take the time to hear what is going on in one another's lives and to pray for one another. Here are some creative ideas I have learned from others to help keep prayer time fresh:

- As women enter the room, direct them to take an index card or sticky note and write their prayer request on it. Then during prayer time, each woman can read her request aloud, already having thought through it, and pass it to the woman on the right for her to keep in her Bible as a reminder to pray for the request until they meet again.
- Ask someone to record all the prayer requests and e-mail them to the group each week.
- If you have a small group, use a one- or two-minute hourglass when you are short on time. (Look in your game closet for one of these.) You can also feel free to use a timer, stopwatch, or a smartphone to monitor the time. Lightheartedly tell each woman that she has one or two minutes to share her request so that each woman can have a turn. (You might want to flip it over again if tears accompany the request.)
- If you have more than ten women, divide into two or three groups for prayer time. Assign a leader who will facilitate, keep the group on track, and follow up. Sometimes our prayer group has gone out for breakfast together or gathered in someone's home to watch the teaching video again.

- Have women pick one or two partners and split into small groups of two or three to share prayer requests and pray for one another.
- Have an open time of "popcorn" prayer. This means letting women spontaneously pray one-sentence prayers as they feel led.
- After everyone shares requests, ask each woman to pray silently for the woman on her right.
- Another option is to close the group in prayer yourself or ask a few women whom you know are comfortable praying in front of others to pray for the requests mentioned. Remember that many women feel awkward praying in front of others. Provide encouragement by reminding the group that prayer is talking to God and that there is no right or wrong way to have a conversation with our Creator. But always be sensitive to others and affirm that they will not be judged if they don't like to pray out loud.

Making a change in your prayer time keeps it from becoming stale or boring. Talking with Jesus should be fresh and real. Taking an intentional, thoughtful approach to this important time of your study will add great value to your time together.

Challenge #4: Developing Leaders

Women's Bible study groups are a great avenue for fulfilling the 2-2-2 principle, which comes from 2 Timothy 2:2: "You have heard me teach things that have been confirmed by many reliable witnesses. Now teach these truths to other trustworthy people who will be able to pass them on to others." As a leader, God calls us to help raise up other leaders.

Is there a woman in your group who is capable of leading? How can you come along-side her and help equip her to be an even better leader? Wonderful women have invested in me through the 2-2-2 principle, even before I knew that term. As an apprentice, I watched them lead. They gave me opportunities to try leading without handing the full reins over to me. Then they coached and corrected me. I have since had the privilege of mentoring several apprentices in my Bible study group and watching them go on to lead their own groups. This is multiplying leaders and groups, and God loves it!

Here is the 2-2-2 principle as laid out by Dave Ferguson and Jon Ferguson in their book *Exponential*.[1] (My notes are added within the brackets.)

- I DO. You WATCH. We TALK.
- I DO. You HELP. We TALK. [Have your apprentice lead a prayer group or an activity or portion of the session.]
- You DO. I HELP. We TALK. [Ask your apprentice to lead one session with you assisting with facilitation alongside her.]
- You DO. I WATCH. We TALK. [Give your apprentice full ownership for leading a session and resist the urge to jump in and take over.]
- You DO. Someone else WATCHES. [As God leads over time, encourage your apprentice to start her own Bible study group.]

My mentor and I led a Bible study group together for years. As the group grew larger, we both sensed God leading us to multiply the group, forming two groups. It was painful as we missed studying and working with each other. However, God blessed and used both groups to reach more women. Then a woman in my group felt called to lead her own study. She worried that no one would come to her group. She asked many questions as we worked through the 2-2-2 principle. Her first group meeting included eighteen women who now, five years later, still love meeting together. I've seen pictures of them on Facebook enjoying special times together, and I praise God for all that He is doing.

From our one study, there are now over five groups of women that meet regularly to study God's Word. This kind of growth begins with commitment to share leadership, follow the 2-2-2 principle, and multiply so that more women can grow in their walk with Christ. Don't miss the opportunity to develop new leaders with intentionality as you model and encourage other women to use their gifts.

Challenge #5: Reaching Out

How do you welcome new women into the group? This is especially tough if yours is an ongoing group that has had the same women in it for years. Newcomers can feel like outsiders if it seems like everyone already knows the unspoken rules of the group. Also, what about those who are finding their way back to God? Are they welcome in the group? While the purpose of the group is primarily Bible study, I've seen the Great Commission of making disciples happen many times through women's groups that meet for Bible study. God's Word will do the transforming work in their lives through the Holy Spirit. We are called to reach out by investing and inviting. Here are some ways a leader can help create an open group:

- End each Bible study with a closing celebration brunch, encouraging the women to bring food and friends. Some ideas for this time together include:
    1. Have an open time when women can share how God worked in their lives through the Bible study.
    2. Have one woman in the group share her testimony of how she came to understand the gospel and how it has been transforming her life recently.
    3. Bring in a speaker from outside the group to share a testimony.
    4. Make it fun! We play a fun group game (such as Fishbowl, Pictionary, or Loaded Questions) and have a white elephant jewelry exchange at Christmas. Women who might think Bible study is a foreign concept can see that you are just a bunch of regular women in pursuit of a supernatural God.

- Though the main purpose of the group is Bible study, consider doing a service project together and invite other women to participate (schedules permitting). Our group has made personal care bags for the homeless and also adopted a family at Christmas, which included going shopping for the gifts and wrapping them together. Depending on where God is leading your group, serving together can help put hands and feet to the truths you are learning.

- While the focus of your group is much more than social, planning an occasional fun event outside of Bible study time can be a good way to forge deeper connections. Our Bible study group has gone bowling together, had a backyard barbecue, and planned a girls' night out at a local restaurant. These times together not only help women get to know one another better but also give women a great chance to invite friends. These same friends who attend a social event might later try a Bible study session once they have made connections with some of the women in the group.

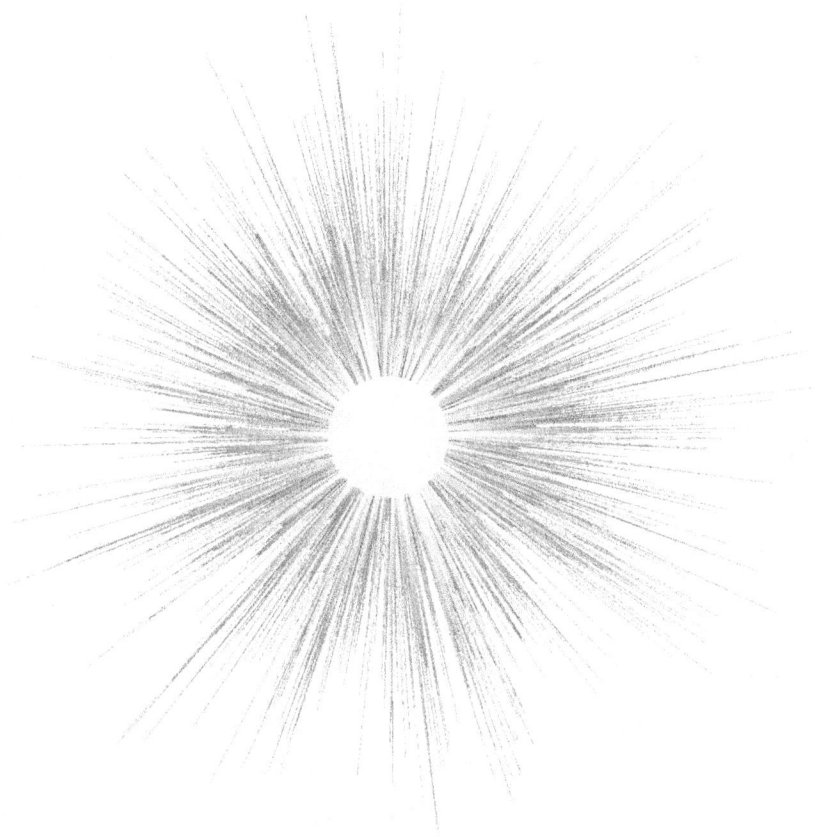

Basic Leader Helps

Preparing for the Sessions

- Check out your meeting space before each group session. Make sure the room is ready. Do you have enough chairs? Do you have the equipment and supplies you need? (See the list of materials needed in each session outline.)
- Pray for your group and each group member by name. Ask God to work in the life of every woman in your group.
- Read and complete the week's readings in the participant workbook and review the session outline in the leader guide. Put a check mark beside the discussion questions you want to cover, and in the margins, make notes about information or insights you want to share in your discussion time.

Leading the Sessions

- Personally greet each woman as she arrives. If desired, take attendance using your group roster. (This will assist you in identifying members who have missed several sessions so that you may contact them and let them know they were missed.)
- At the start of each session, ask the women to turn off or silence their cell phones.
- Always start on time. Honor the efforts of those who are on time.
- Encourage everyone to participate fully, but don't put anyone on the spot. Invite the women to share as they are comfortable. Be prepared to offer a personal example or answer if no one else responds at first.

- Facilitate but don't dominate. If you talk most of the time, group members may tend to listen passively rather than engage personally.
- Try not to interrupt, judge, or minimize anyone's comments or input.
- Remember that you are not expected to be the expert or have all the answers. Acknowledge that all of you are on this journey together, with the Holy Spirit as your leader and guide. If issues or questions arise that you don't feel equipped to answer or handle, it's OK to say "I don't know." Talk with the pastor or a staff member at your church and circle back with the women later to share what you discovered.
- Encourage good discussion, but don't be timid about calling time on a particular question and moving ahead. Part of your responsibility is to keep the group on track. If you decide to spend extra time on a given question or activity, consider skipping or spending less time on another question or activity in order to stay on schedule.
- Try to end on time. If you are running over, give members the opportunity to leave if they need to. Then wrap up as quickly as you can.
- Be prepared for some women to want to hang out and talk at the end. If you need everyone to leave by a certain time, communicate this at the beginning of the session. If you are meeting in a church during regularly scheduled activities or have arranged for childcare, be sensitive to the agreed-upon ending time.
- Thank the women for coming, and let them know you're looking forward to seeing them next time.

Introductory Session

Note: The regular session outline has been modified for this optional introductory session, which is 60 minutes long.

Leader Prep

Materials Needed

- *Acts* DVD and DVD player or equipment to stream the video online
- stick-on name tags and markers (optional)
- index card (optional—Prayer Requests)
- participant workbooks to purchase or distribute

Session Outline

Note: Refer to the format templates on pages 7–8 for suggested time allotments.

Welcome

Offer a word of welcome to the group. If time allows and you choose to provide food, invite the women to enjoy refreshments and fellowship. (Groups meeting for 60 minutes may want to have a time for food and fellowship before the official start time.) Be sure to watch the clock and move to the All Play icebreaker at the appropriate time.

All Play

Ask group members to complete this phrase: "To help me awaken each day, I must

_____." (It doesn't have to be a deep theological answer, perhaps "have coffee or a hot shower"!)

Distribute the participant workbooks, and then have the group turn to the introduction. Point out the different options for study (page 7–8 of the participant workbook) and encourage each woman to prayerfully decide which level of study she would like to complete.

Prayer/Video

Ask God to prepare the group to be receptive and hear His voice. Play the Introductory Video.

Group Discussion

Discuss:

- What part of the video introduction piqued your interest?
- Read Acts 1:8 together. (Page 10 of the participant workbook.)
- How does the task of being a witness to the good news of Jesus awaken you to action?
- What do you hope to discover from this study?

Prayer Requests

End by inviting group members to share prayer requests and pray for one another. Use index cards, popcorn prayer, or another prayer technique included in "Tips for Tackling Five Common Challenges" (pages 13–19) to lead this time with intentionality and sensitivity.

Week 1

Awakening to God's Power

Acts 1–4

Leader Prep

Memory Verse

"But you will receive power when the Holy Spirit comes upon you. And you will be my witnesses, telling people about me everywhere—in Jerusalem, throughout Judea, in Samaria, and to the ends of the earth."

(Acts 1:8)

Materials Needed

- *Acts* DVD and DVD player or equipment to stream the video online
- stick-on name tags and markers (optional)
- index cards or sticky notes (optional—Scriptures and Prayer Requests)

Session Outline

Note: Refer to the format templates on pages 7–8 for suggested time allotments.

Welcome

Offer a word of welcome to the group. If time allows and you choose to provide food, invite the women to enjoy refreshments and fellowship. (Groups meeting for 60 minutes may want to have a time for food and fellowship before the official start time.) Be sure to watch the clock and move to the All Play icebreaker at the appropriate time.

All Play

Ask each group member to respond briefly to the following prompt:

- If you could have a special superpower, what would it be?

After everyone has shared, **say something like this**:

> It's fun to think of fun superpowers, isn't it? In this session, we read how the early Christ-followers awaken to God's power as the Holy Spirit makes a grand entrance on the day of Pentecost. Ordinary people can be used in extraordinary ways when God's power flows through them. Pause and think about that sentence. Many days we feel so ordinary, doing ordinary tasks, going through the motions of our daily living. Through God's Spirit, we can allow God to use us to serve, love, and share the good news of Jesus. Now, that's pretty extraordinary!

Prayer/Video

Ask God to prepare the group to receive His Word and hear His voice. Play the video for Week 1. Invite participants to complete the Video Viewer Guide for Week 1 in the participant workbook (page 43) as they watch. (Answers are provided on page 61 of this leader guide and page 207 of the participant workbook.)

Group Discussion

Video Discussion Questions

- God is all powerful. How does it make you feel to know that even in your seasons of feeling powerless, God is present in your lives?

- How can we awaken to God's Spirit for our everyday lives?
- How does having an active prayer life with God deepen the spiritual rhythms in your everyday life?
- Let's say Acts 1:8 together. Describe ways this verse awakens you to serve and share.

PARTICIPANT WORKBOOK DISCUSSION QUESTIONS

Note: Page references are provided for those questions that relate to questions or activities in the participant workbook.

Before you begin, invite volunteers to look up the following Scriptures and be prepared to read them aloud when called upon. You might want to write each of the Scripture references on a separate index card or sticky note that you can hand out.

Scriptures: Galatians 5:22-23; Acts 3:6-7

Day 1: The Power of the Pen (Introduction)

- Who wrote the Book of Acts?
- Luke was a fascinating person. Describe him.
- Why were Luke's investigative skills so vital to the development of the Book of Acts?
- What did people use as sources for written accounts of Jesus and the early church? Why are these written accounts so important for us today?
- Ask if a few individuals would be willing to share a personal takeaway from Session 1. See page 16.

Day 2: Power in the Promise (Acts 1)

- Think of the last promise you made to someone. How does it make you feel knowing that God keeps His promises during our seasons of waiting?
- During your most recent season of waiting, how did the power of God sustain you?

- In Acts 1:14, what do we find Jesus's followers doing? Prayer united and prepared them as they waited for the promised Holy Spirit. (page 21)
- Why is prayer so important to our Christian living? What do you feel praying accomplishes?
- Ask if a few individuals would be willing to share how they completed the question about their current prayer life. (Page 21)
- Where did you see God at work in Acts 1?

Day 3: Power in the Holy Spirit (Acts 2)

- Our reading from Acts 2:1-13 tells of many powerful happenings. Try to imagine you were an eyewitness on the day of Pentecost. Ask group members to describe the sights, colors, and sounds around them.
- Have someone read aloud Galatians 5:22-23. How has the experience of God's supernatural fruit transformed relationships with others? (page 25)
- In Acts 2:38, Peter told the people present they were to do several things before they received the Holy Spirit. Name them.
- What is a way you observed God at work in Acts 2? (page 28)
- Where did you see God at work in Acts 2?

Day 4: Power in the Name of Jesus (Acts 3)

- Think of a time you were with a group of people. Was anyone in the group a name-dropper? How did it make you feel when all these names were mentioned?
- In Acts 3, we discover the power of name-dropping for every Christ-follower. Who were the disciples in action in verses 1-11?
- What did the crippled man want from Peter and John? What did he receive instead? (page 30)
- Have someone read Acts 3:6-7. Where was the power? Jesus's name has power!
- In verses 12-26, we read how Peter used this time as an opportunity to preach. What did Peter tell the people to do in verse 19?
- Where did you see God at work in Acts 3?

Day 5: Power in Prayer (Acts 4)

- In Acts 4:1-22, we discover that many people were not pleased with the actions of Peter and John. Imagine you have just been hired to cover this story. How would you report these happenings? (Have others add their accounts to the story.)
- Powerful prayers in Scripture often start by praising God and recognizing God's position of authority. Why do you feel praising God is essential in your prayer life?
- Think of a favorite friend or family member and how much you love talking with them. Now, think about God. God wants to have a close relationship with you. What keeps you from having that close relationship with God and praying more often?
- Where did you see God at work in Acts 4?

Optional Group Activity (for a session longer than 60 minutes)

Before the session begins, place a large sheet of paper on a wall. Using a colorful, washable marker, write out the numbers 1 through 5 on the paper. Make sure each person has a marker and a small pad of sticky notes. Call their attention to the Weekly Wrap-Up (page 42). Ask each member to write out their Personal Application responses on the sticky notes then place them on the wall by the corresponding numbers. Have each person walk around and read the various responses. Thank them for their participation in the activity.

Prayer Requests

Invite the group members to share prayer requests and pray for one another. Use index cards or sticky notes, popcorn prayer, or another prayer technique included in "Tips for Tackling Five Common Challenges" (pages 13–19) to lead this time with intentionality and sensitivity.

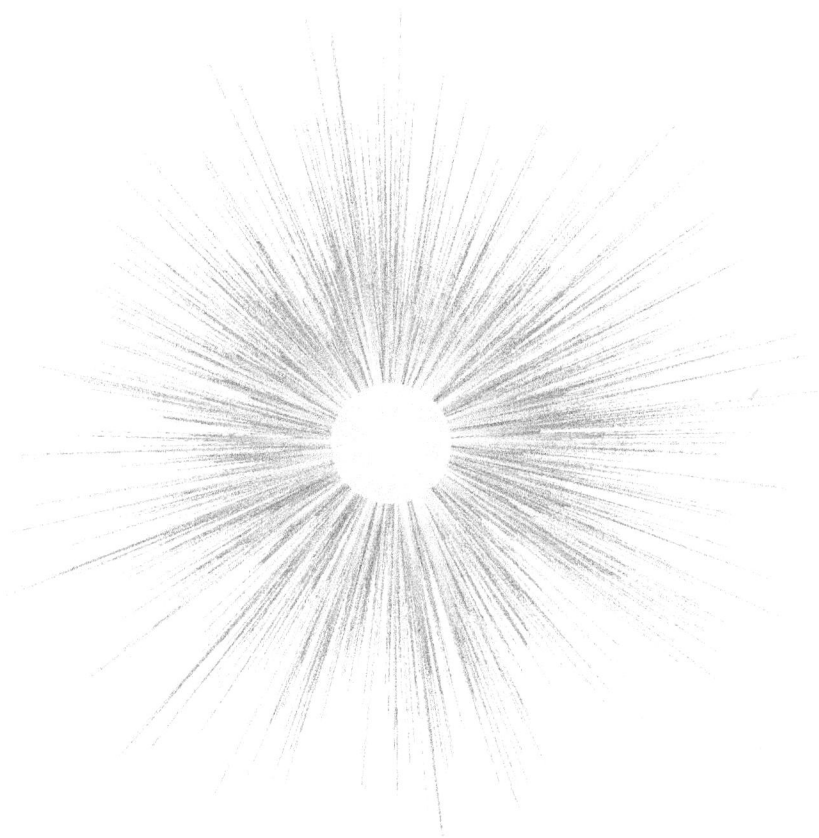

Week 2

Awakening to God's Message

Acts 5–9

Leader Prep

Memory Verse

And every day, in the Temple and from house to house, they continued to teach and preach this message: "Jesus is the Messiah."

(Acts 5:42)

Materials Needed

- Acts DVD and DVD player or equipment to stream the video online
- stick-on name tags and markers (optional)
- index cards or sticky notes (optional—Scriptures and Prayer Requests)

Session Outline

Note: Refer to the format templates on pages 7–8 for suggested time allotments.

Welcome

Offer a word of welcome to the group. If time allows and you choose to provide food, invite the women to enjoy refreshments and fellowship. (Groups meeting for 60 minutes may want to have a time for food and fellowship before the official start time.) Be sure to watch the clock and move to the All Play icebreaker at the appropriate time.

All Play

Ask each group member to respond briefly to the following prompt. Read aloud or paraphrase:

- What TV show, game, or activity distracts you from your Bible study time?

  Say: God desires time and fellowship with each one of us. And He is the one and only who really matters!

Prayer/Video

Ask God to prepare the group to receive His Word and hear His voice. Play the video for Week 2. Invite participants to complete the Video Viewer Guide for Week 2 in the participant workbook (page 73) as they watch. (Answers are provided on page 61 of this leader guide and page 207 of the participant workbook.)

Group Discussion

VIDEO DISCUSSION QUESTIONS

- How do you respond to disturbances in your life?
- What does awakening to God's message mean to you?
- How does John 3:16 shape the message from God for our lives?
- Why do you feel we hide the messes in our lives from others?

- Where do you see God working in your life?

Note: Page references are provided for those questions that relate to questions or activities in the participant workbook.

Before you begin, notice who has various translations of the Bible. Invite volunteers to look up Acts 9:15 and be prepared to read it aloud when called upon. You might want to write each of the Scripture references on a separate index card or sticky note that you can hand out.

Scripture: Acts 5:42

Day 1: The Message of Life (Acts 5)

- Stop and think of some of the excuses you have used to avoid quality time with God in prayer and Bible study. How can our excuses and time away from God lead to issues with our Christian living?
- Whose praise were Ananias and Sapphira seeking? Describe what happens because of their behavior. (page 46)
- Why do you feel Luke included this story in this chapter? (page 46)
- Why is the message given by Gamaliel in verses 38-39 so vital for our Christian living?
- Read aloud together the memory verse from Acts 5:42. The good news of God's message leads to _____. (page 44)

Day 2: The Priority of the Message (Acts 6)

- From our readings in Acts 6, explore the reasons we must prioritize the teaching of God's Word. (page 52)
- In verses 1-7 we discover rumblings of discontent in the church. What was the main issue for this discontent? (page 50)
- What was the plan of action that was used to address this issue?

- What are some takeaways we find in verses 1-7? How do these answers compare to the church and our world today? (page 51)
- Where did you see God at work in Acts 6?

Day 3: Context for the Message (Acts 7)

- Describe a time when hearing a backstory helped shift the way you thought or felt about something. (page 54)
- Why do you think Stephen went into such detail highlighting passages from the Old Testament?
- Imagine you are interviewing Stephen. What questions would you ask him?
- What was the result of Stephen's commitment to the truth and the message of the good news of Jesus?
- Where did you see God at work in Acts 7?

Day 4: Personal Messages (Acts 8)

- Have someone read Acts 1:8. How is this verse applicable to our study in Acts 8?
- What happens as a result of Stephen's death?
- What empowered the early Christians to keep praying and sharing the gospel?
- Ask if a few individuals would be willing to share their story when they first sensed the work of the Holy Spirit in their lives.
- Often we might feel unworthy to share the good news of Jesus with one another. Thankfully Philip responded to God's call. How did he make a difference?
- Where did you see God at work in Acts 8?

Day 5: The Life-Changing Message (Acts 9)

- In Acts 9:3-9, we discover Saul's powerful encounter with Jesus. Describe what happened. (page 66)
- Saul had an awakening to God's message. How did he respond to this life-changing message?

- How has your encounter with Jesus awakened you to seek and share God's message?
- In Acts 9:32-43, God uses Peter as His instrument or agent. Describe what happened.
- Where did you see God at work in Acts 9?

Optional Group Activity (for a session longer than 60 minutes)

Divide into smaller groups or pairs to review the Weekly Wrap-Up (page 72). Ask small groups to share and discuss their wrap-up statements and one or two ways they will put into practice something they discovered from Acts 9.

Prayer Requests

Invite the group members to share prayer requests and pray for one another. Use index cards or sticky notes, popcorn prayer, or another prayer technique included in "Tips for Taking Five Common Challenges" (pages 13–19) to lead this time with intentionality and sensitivity.

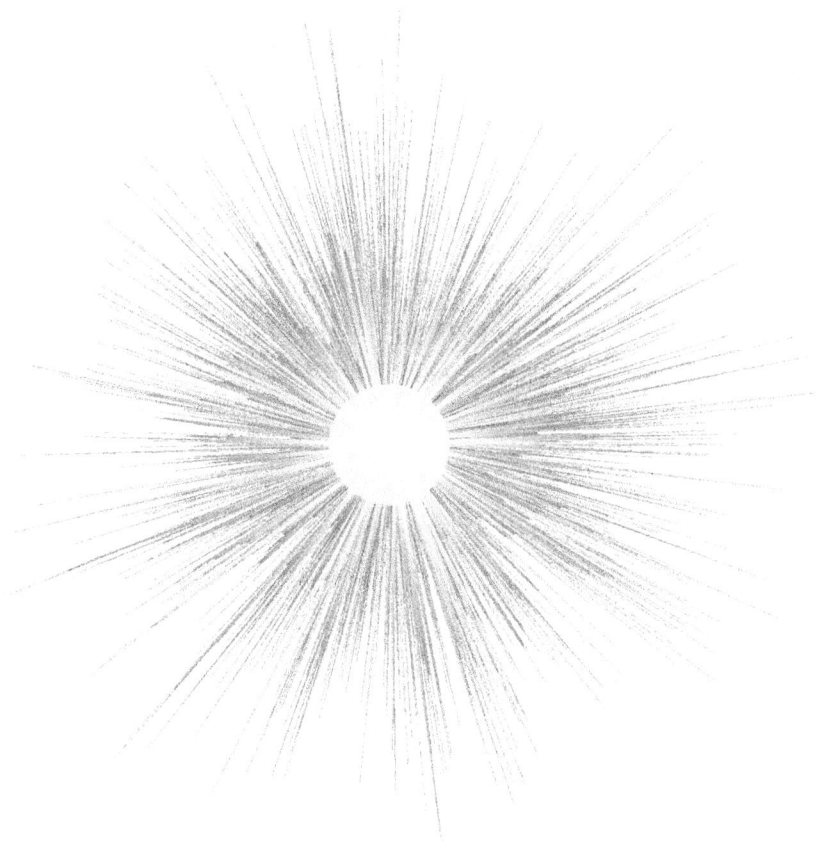

Week 3

Awakening to God's Freedom

Acts 10–14

Leader Prep

Memory Verse

Then Peter replied, 'I see very clearly that God shows no favoritism. In every nation he accepts those who fear him and do what is right. This is the message of Good News for the people of Israel—that there is peace with God through Jesus Christ, who is Lord of all."

(Acts 10:34-36)

Materials Needed

- Acts DVD and DVD player or equipment to stream the video online
- stick-on name tags and markers (optional)
- index cards or sticky notes (optional—Scriptures and Prayer Requests)

Session Outline

Note: Refer to the format templates on pages 7–8 for suggested time allotments.

Welcome

Offer a word of welcome to the group. If time allows and you choose to provide food, invite the women to enjoy refreshments and fellowship. (Groups meeting for 60 minutes may want to have a time for food and fellowship before the official start time.) Be sure to watch the clock and move to the All Play icebreaker at the appropriate time.

All Play

Ask each group member to respond briefly to the following prompt. Read aloud or paraphrase:

- What's the most embarrassing fashion trend you wore while in school? Did you wear it to be part of the cool group in school?

  After everyone has shared, **say**:

  During our study we discover that God accepts and loves all of His children. What a comfort it is knowing that we are loved and valued by God.

Prayer/Video

Ask God to prepare the group to receive His Word and hear His voice. Play the video for Week 3. Invite participants to complete the Video Viewer Guide for Week 3 in the participant workbook (page 105) as they watch. (Answers are provided on page 61 of this leader guide and page 207 of the participant workbook.)

Group Discussion

VIDEO DISCUSSION QUESTIONS

- If you have had an experience with legalism please share your story with the group.

- We can't embrace God's freedom until we let go of old bondage. Why is this action sometimes difficult to follow?
- Why does trying to achieve perfection through rule following not work for our lives?
- How can our memory verse become a personal mission statement for us as Christians?
- Where do you see God working in your life?

PARTICIPANT WORKBOOK DISCUSSION QUESTIONS

Note: Page references are provided for those questions that relate to questions or activities in the participant workbook.

Before you begin, invite volunteers to look up the following Scriptures and be prepared to read them aloud when called upon. You might want to write each of the Scripture references on a separate index card or sticky note that you can hand out.

Scriptures: Acts 10:1-16; Acts 10:34-36

Day 1: Freedom from Favoritism (Acts 10)

- Our reading from Acts 10:1-16 describes Cornelius and Peter's visions. How are these visions similar and different? (page 76)
- Imagine you are a reporter for the nightly news. Describe the interaction between Cornelius and Peter. Then ask the group why this interaction was unprecedented in that day and time? (page 77)
- Ask someone to read Acts 10:34-36. Why is Peter's encounter with others so life-changing?
- How can "sitting at a different lunch table" empower us to share the good news of Jesus with everyone?
- Where did you see God at work in Acts 10?

Day 2: Freedom from Tradition (Acts 11)

- What happened in Acts 11:1-18 to change the minds of believers?

- How has your faith in God awakened you to be more discerning?
- Describe your feelings when you hear words such as *requirements* and *preferences* for following Jesus. (page 81)
- Look at verse 26. Why is that verse so important to us as Christ-followers?
- Where did you see God at work in Acts 11?

Day 3: Freedom from Bondage (Acts 12)

- Why did King Herod have Peter put in prison?
- After reading the passage from Hebrews 11:33-38, how did you respond to the question about the relationship between faithfulness and "circumstantial freedom"?
- Describe how Herod's freedom ended.
- Imagine you were asked to write a short blog post and your topic is "What does freedom in Christ look like to you?" What would you write?
- Where did you see God at work in Acts 12?

Day 4: Freedom to Share (Acts 13)

- Refer to Acts 13:1-3. How did the Holy Spirit speak to the believers in the early church?
- In Acts 13:43, Paul and Barnabas urged new believers to be faithful to the message of God's grace. Why does that message still apply to us today?
- How is it possible to have joy in Christ during good and not-so-good times?
- Reflect on your freedom in Christ. How does having this freedom motivate you to share the good news with others?
- Where did you see God at work in Acts 13?

Day 5: Freedom to Focus (Acts 14)

- Have you ever been with someone who wasn't really listening to you? How do you think God feels when we don't focus on God's Word and time with God?
- How did the Holy Spirit transform Paul and Barnabas during their travels in Acts 14?

- We discover in Acts 14:23 the appointment of elders. Why were elders important in the life of the early church?
- How does awakening to God's freedom help us find the power to change our focus?
- Where did you see God at work in Acts 14?

Optional Group Activity (for a session longer than 60 minutes)

Divide into smaller groups or pairs to review the Weekly Wrap-Up (page 104). Ask small groups to share and discuss their wrap-up statements and one or two ways they will put into practice something they learned from their readings this week.

Prayer Requests

Invite the group members to share prayer requests and pray for one another. Use index cards or sticky notes, popcorn prayer, or another prayer technique included in "Tips for Tackling Five Common Challenges" (pages 13–19) to lead this time with intentionality and sensitivity.

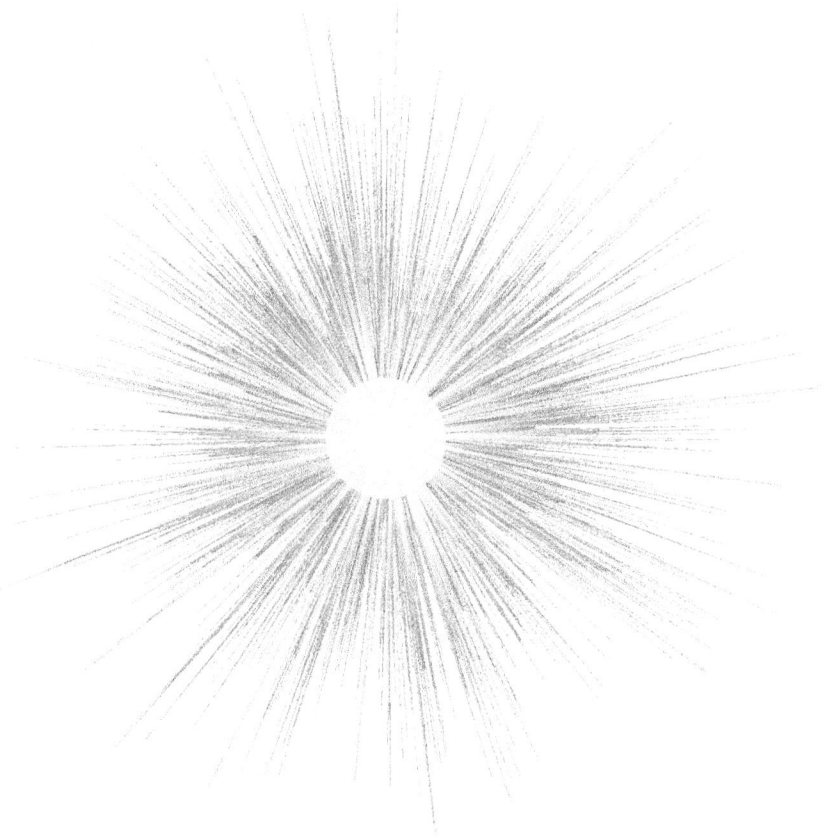

Week 4

Awakening to God's Grace

Acts 15–19

Leader Prep

Memory Verse

> *"We believe that we are all saved the same way, by the undeserved grace of the Lord Jesus."*
>
> (Acts 15:11)

Materials Needed

- *Acts* DVD and DVD player or equipment to stream the video online
- stick-on name tags and markers (optional)
- index cards or sticky notes (optional—Scriptures and Prayer Requests)

Session Outline

Note: Refer to the format templates on pages 7–8 for suggested time allotments.

Welcome

Offer a word of welcome to the group. If time allows and you choose to provide food, invite the women to enjoy refreshments and fellowship. (Groups meeting for 60 minutes may want to have a time for food and fellowship before the official start time.) Be sure to watch the clock and move to the All Play icebreaker at the appropriate time.

All Play

Ask each group member to respond briefly to the following prompt. Read aloud or paraphrase:

- If you could be a season what would you be?

    Say: The various seasons of the year awaken our senses and hopes to new ideas and possibilities. As we prepare to listen and learn, let's give thanks to God for all the wonders of each season.

Prayer/Video

Ask God to prepare the group to receive His Word and hear His voice. Play the video for Week 4. Invite participants to complete the Video Viewer Guide for Week 4 in the participant workbook (page 138) as they watch. (Answers are provided on page 61 of this leader guide and page 207 of the participant workbook.)

Group Discussion

VIDEO DISCUSSION QUESTIONS

- After studying Acts 15–19, what feelings or thoughts come to mind when you hear the term *grace*?
- How can we awaken to God through disagreements with others in our daily life and those in our churches?
- Where was the grace of God during the time that Paul and Barnabas went their separate ways in ministry?
- Where do you see God working in your life?

PARTICIPANT WORKBOOK DISCUSSION QUESTIONS

Note: Page references are provided for those questions that relate to questions or activities in the participant workbook.

Before you begin, ask your participants to read the memory verse, Acts 15:11, to themselves. Select someone in advance to read Acts 16:27-28 out loud.

Scriptures: Acts 15:11; Acts 16:27-28; Acts 19:9

Day 1: Grace to Disagree (Acts 15)

- Read Acts 15:11 out loud together. Describe the phrase "underserved grace of the Lord Jesus."
- Review Acts 15:36-41. Why did Paul and Barnabas disagree?
- How does being a Christ-follower equip us to have the grace to disagree?
- Why are listening and learning valuable skills in conflict management?
- Where did you see God at work in Acts 15?

Day 2: Grace to Show Deference (Acts 16)

- In Acts 16:1-5, we discover an example of deference or respect. Describe a time when you valued relationships over rules.
- Refer to Acts 16:11-15. Why is Lydia a role model for us as women today?
- In Acts 16, we find Paul and Silas praying and singing at midnight. During tough times, what is a song, hymn, or Bible passage that God calls to your mind to use to comfort and reassure you? (page 116)
- Ask someone to read aloud Acts 16:27-28. Why do you think Paul and Silas remained in place in prison even after the doors were opened?
- Where did you see God at work in Acts 16?

Day 3: Grace to Keep an Open Mind (Acts 17)

- Why does keeping an open mind while studying the Scriptures allow for new ideas with discernment?

- When we hear others discuss Bible passages, why is it important for us to do our own research and study?
- In Acts 17, we meet the Bereans. Describe their values and beliefs. What can we learn and apply in our own lives from the Bereans? (page 121)
- Refer to Acts 17:16-34. Name ways Paul used his own creativity and open-mindedness to relate the gospel to the Athenians.
- Where did you see God at work in Acts 17?

Day 4: Partners in Grace (Acts 18)

- Refer to Proverbs 13:20. Why is having wise friends important for us as women?
- Ask someone to read aloud Acts 18:15. Silas and Timothy gave Paul encouragement. How can you be an encourager to leaders in your church?
- Describe the leadership skills of Priscilla and Aquila. How were those skills an asset to Paul?
- Think about your partners in grace and their characteristics. How do those characteristics make them such dear partners in grace?
- Where did you see God at work in Acts 18?

Day 5: The Eyes of Grace (Acts 19)

- Where have you encountered God's grace in unexpected places or situations? (page 131)
- Refer to Acts 19:1-7. Why is it important for us to have a deeper understanding of what it means to be a true follower of Christ?
- Have someone read Acts 19:9. What actions taken by the crowd caused Paul to leave the synagogue?
- Think of a time in your spiritual journey when friends and coworkers closed their minds to the gospel. Describe the pain it brought you.
- Name ways we as Christians can equip ourselves to discover cultural counterfeits in our midst.
- Where did you see God at work in Acts 19?

Optional Group Activity (for a session longer than 60 minutes)

Divide into smaller groups or pairs to review the Weekly Wrap-Up (page 137). Ask small groups to share and discuss their wrap-up statements and one or two ways that they will put into practice something they learned from their readings this week.

Prayer Requests

Invite the group members to share prayer requests and pray for one another. Use index cards or sticky notes, popcorn prayer, or another prayer technique included in "Tips for Tackling Five Common Challenges" (pages 13–19) to lead this time with intentionality and sensitivity.

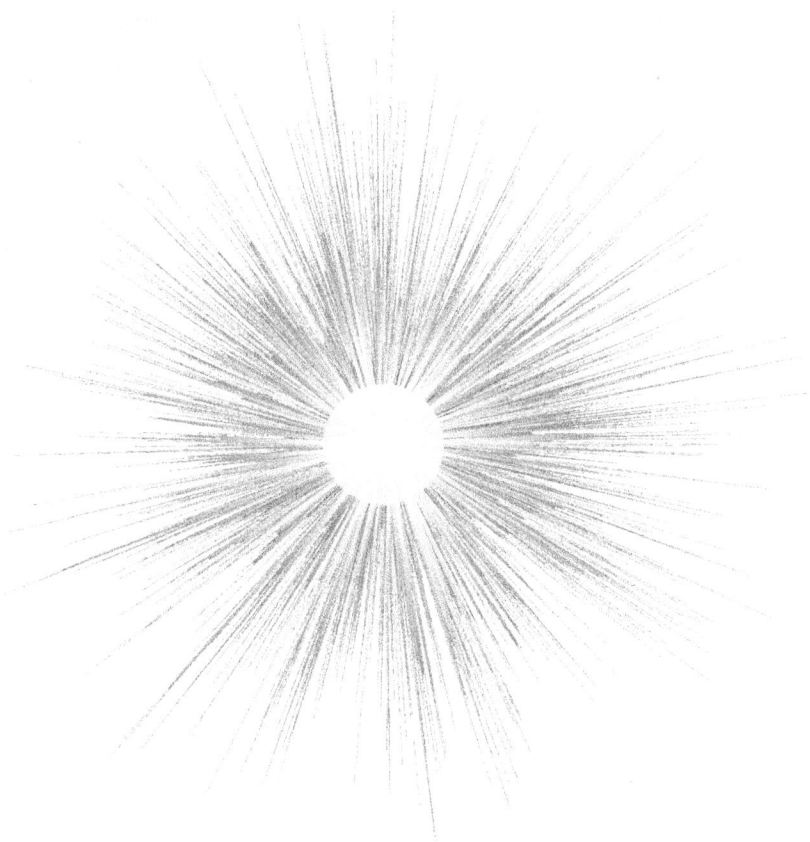

Week 5

Awakening to God's Mission

Acts 20–24

Leader Prep

Memory Verse

"But my life is worth nothing to me unless I use it for finishing the work assigned me by the Lord Jesus—the work of telling others the Good News about the wonderful grace of God."

(Acts 20:24)

Materials Needed

- Acts DVD and DVD player or equipment to stream the video online
- stick-on name tags and markers (optional)
- index cards or sticky notes (optional—Scriptures and Prayer Requests)

Session Outline

Note: Refer to the format templates on pages 7–8 for suggested time allotments.

Welcome

Offer a word of welcome to the group. If time allows and you choose to provide food, invite the women to enjoy refreshments and fellowship. (Groups meeting for 60 minutes may want to have a time for food and fellowship before the official start time.) Be sure to watch the clock and move to the All Play icebreaker at the appropriate time.

All Play

Ask each group member to respond briefly to the following prompt:

- What is something we probably don't know about you?

After everyone shares, **say**:

It's fun to discover new things about one another. Making new discoveries about one another and our world awakens us to new possibilities for learning and growing.

Prayer/Video

Ask God to prepare the group to receive His Word and hear His voice. Play the video for Week 5. Invite participants to complete the Video Viewer Guide for Week 5 in the participant workbook (page 169) as they watch. (Answers are provided on page 61 of this leader guide and page 207 of the participant workbook.)

Group Discussion

VIDEO DISCUSSION QUESTIONS

- God has a purpose for your life and for mine. How does it make you feel knowing you are special and unique and God loves you?
- What was Paul's target? Describe ways he kept his focus on that bull's-eye.
- Think about how faithful Philip was in his service to God. How does his example awaken us to share the good news of Jesus?

- How can you rely on God as you awaken to His mission with greater dependency?
- Picture your daily life. Describe ways are you living a faith-filled life.

PARTICIPANT WORKBOOK DISCUSSION QUESTIONS

Note: Page references are provided for those questions that relate to questions or activities in the participant workbook.

Before you begin, invite volunteers to look up the following Scriptures and be prepared to read them aloud when called upon. You might want to write each of the Scripture references on a separate index card or sticky note that you can hand out.

Scriptures: Acts 20:2; Acts 23:11; Psalm 27:14

Day 1: A Mission Worth the Sacrifices (Acts 20)

- A disciple is associated with being a learner. Why is learning a lifelong skill for us as Christians?
- What are some challenges you have faced either in the past or present as you heeded Jesus's call to make disciples? (page 143)
- Reflect on Matthew 28:18-20. How do these verses inspire you to equip disciples?
- Ask someone to read aloud Acts 20:21. If you were to create a mission statement for your life what would it be?
- Think about all the sacrifices made by Paul. Now, think of your sacrifices. What can we learn from Paul's life as a disciple?
- Where did you see God at work in Acts 20?

Day 2: Misunderstanding and the Mission (Acts 21)

- Imagine you are an eyewitness to the events in Acts 21:1-14. Describe what happened.
- What made Paul's conviction regarding his travels to Jerusalem so strong?

- How can we as Christian women use the principles outlined in Scripture and in our study concerning relationships and misunderstandings to guide our hearts in our daily lives?
- Briefly describe what happened to Paul in Acts 21:26-40. (page 149)
- Where did you see God at work in Acts 21?

Day 3: Simplifying the Mission (Acts 22)

- Reflect on the passage in Acts 22:1-23. Now, imagine you are Paul and have been called on to give your testimony at a Sunday night service. What would you say?
- Ask several participants to share how they have seen God at work recently in their lives. (page 152)
- In Acts 22:24-30, why was Paul's citizenship an issue?
- Why do you feel an awakening to God's mission happens when we share our personal story of our faith in Jesus?
- Where did you see God at work in Acts 22?

Day 4: Encouragement in Mission (Acts 23)

- Review Acts 23:1-10. Name some of the human reactions displayed by Paul. (page 156)
- Have someone read aloud Acts 23:11. How do you think Paul felt when Jesus told him to take courage and be encouraged?
- What promises in the Bible encourage you? Describe the comfort of these promises. (page 158)
- Imagine you are Paul's sister. Think of ways you could be an encourager for Paul.
- Where did you see God at work in Acts 23?

Day 5: Pressing Pause on the Mission (Acts 24)

- Paul stated his defense for Felix. Summarize that defense. (page 162)
- Reflect on Acts 24:14-16. How does this passage awaken you?

- Ask someone to read aloud Psalm 27:14. (Use the NRSV or NIV translation.) Waiting on God is an active process. Describe ways we wait on God.
- What awakening do you think Paul experienced during his season of waiting?
- Where did you see God at work in Acts 24?

Optional Group Activity (for a session longer than 60 minutes)

Divide into smaller groups or pairs to review the Weekly Wrap-Up (page 168). Ask small groups to share and discuss their wrap-up statements and one or two ways that they will put into practice something they learned from their readings this week.

Prayer Requests

Invite the group members to share prayer requests and pray for one another. Use index cards or sticky notes, popcorn prayer, or another prayer technique included in "Tips for Tackling Five Common Challenges" (pages 13–19) to lead this time with intentionality and sensitivity.

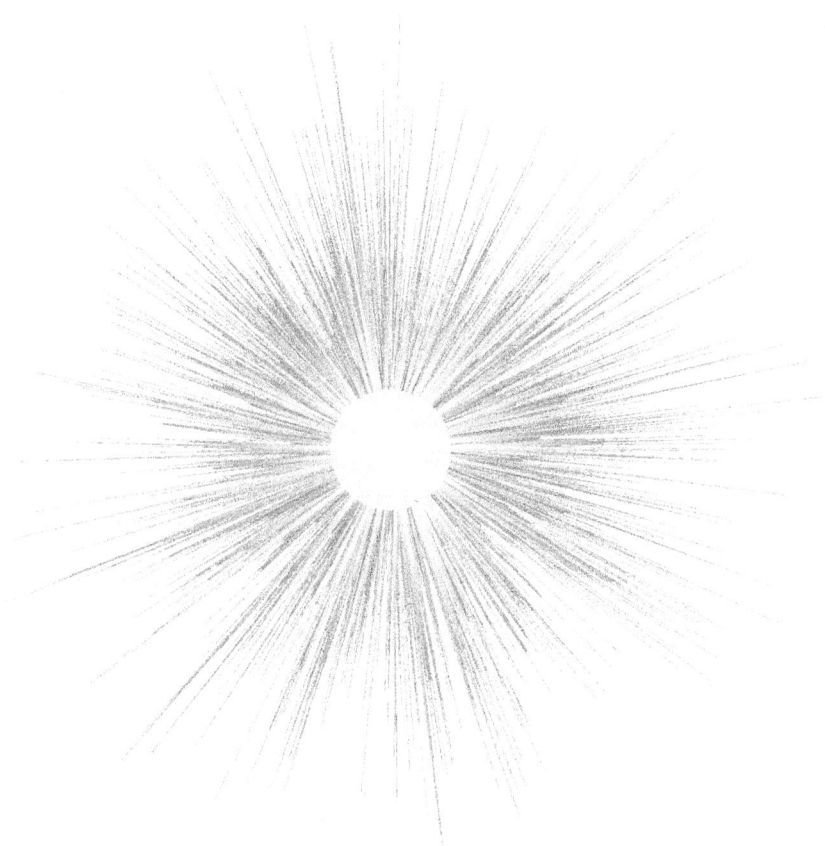

Week 6

Awakening to God's Direction

Acts 25–28

Leader Prep

Memory Verse

"'And I will rescue you from both your own people and the Gentiles. Yes, I am sending you to the Gentiles to open their eyes, so they may turn from darkness to light and from the power of Satan to God. Then they will receive forgiveness for their sins and be given a place among God's people, who are set apart by faith in me.'"

(Acts 26:17-18)

Materials Needed

- Acts DVD and DVD player or equipment to stream the video online
- stick-on name tags and markers (optional)
- index cards or sticky notes (optional—Scriptures and Prayer Requests)

- blank cardstock bookmarks
- gel pens
- sun shapes or star stickers

Session Outline

Note: Refer to the format templates on pages 7–8 for suggested time allotments.

Welcome

Offer a word of welcome to the group. If time allows and you choose to provide food, invite the women to enjoy refreshments and fellowship. (Groups meeting for 60 minutes may want to have a time for food and fellowship before the official start time.) Be sure to watch the clock and move to the All Play icebreaker at the appropriate time.

All Play

Ask each group member to respond briefly to the following prompt. Read aloud or paraphrase:

- When traveling to a new place, would you rather stop and ask directions from a stranger, use a map app, or phone a friend?

    Say: It's difficult to admit we need help, isn't it? We all need help from time to time as we travel the road of life. Asking God for wisdom is always a great place to start.

Prayer/Video

Ask God to prepare the group to receive His Word and hear His voice. Play the video for Week 6. Invite participants to complete the Video Viewer Guide for Week 6 in the participant workbook as they watch (page 198). (Answers are provided on page 61 of this leader guide and page 207 of the participant workbook.)

Group Discussion

- Describe Paul's doormat posture.
- Jesus is our anchor. Think about the storms in your life. How does having Jesus as an anchor hold our lives together?
- How is God calling you to be a beacon of hope in the midst of your storms?
- How did God awaken you through the study of Acts?
- Repeat Acts 1:8. After our study together, how is God calling you to action?

PARTICIPANT WORKBOOK DISCUSSION QUESTIONS

Note: Page references are provided for those questions that relate to questions or activities in the participant workbook.

Before you begin, invite volunteers to look up the following Scriptures and be prepared to read them aloud when called upon. You might want to write each of the Scripture references on a separate index card or sticky note that you can hand out.

Scriptures: Acts 1:8; Acts 25:18-19; Acts 26:17-18; Acts 27:35-36

Day 1: Direction in Decisions (Acts 25)

- Describe the motivation for the decisions made by Festus.
- Paul was motivated by the good news of Jesus. How does the good news of Jesus motivate you?
- Ask someone to read aloud Acts 25:18-19. Why did this discussion surprise Festus? (page 172)
- How does God direct your decision-making?
- Where did you see God at work in Acts 25?

Day 2: Directed toward God (Acts 26)

- Paul provided a powerful defense. Describe ways Paul directed his listeners to God. (page 178)

- Have someone read aloud Acts 26:17-18. What was Paul commanded to do?
- In what areas of your life can you turn from darkness to light?
- Reflect on Acts 26:29. How does this verse awaken your spirit?
- Where did you see God at work in Acts 26?

Day 3: Boldness in Dangerous Directions (Acts 27)

- God calls us to boldly trust His directions and encourage one other even in the stormiest seasons of life. How can we boldly trust God during the storms of our lives?
- Refer to your notes concerning Acts 27:13-26. Outline the challenges Paul faced. (pages 183–184)
- How did Paul's bold attitude encourage others?
- Have someone read Acts 27:35-36. Even during this dangerous time, Paul stopped and gave thanks to God for their food. What can we learn from this action?
- Where did you see God at work in Acts 27?

Day 4: Directed to Faithfulness (Acts 28)

- Why was the island called Malta memorable for Paul?
- Once Paul was settled in Rome, he called all the Jewish leaders together. What did he tell them? (page 190)
- Why do you feel God calls us to faithfulness as Christians?
- What was Paul's mission in Rome?
- Where did you see God at work in Acts 28?

Day 5: Unstoppable Directions (Review)

- Have someone read aloud Acts 1:8. As we complete our study, how does Acts 1:8 awaken you to serve and share? How does this differ from when we started the study?
- After studying the Book of Acts, describe ways God's unstoppable plan moved forward.
- What transformation has taken place in your life during these six weeks?

- Describe the confidence you have gained to serve and share because of this study.
- What are two key takeaways for you personally from the Book of Acts? (page 197)

Optional Group Activity (for a session longer than 60 minutes)

To close your study, hand out blank cardstock bookmarks and set out some gel pens and stickers. Ask participants to reflect on the memory verses and main points they've studied over the past six weeks and invite them to write on their bookmarks a favorite memory verse, word, or quote from a daily reading. If you have time, ask some volunteers to share what they wrote and why.

Prayer Requests

Invite the group members to share prayer requests and pray for one another. Use index cards or sticky notes, popcorn prayer, or another prayer technique included in "Tips for Tackling Five Common Challenges" (pages 13–19) to lead this time with intentionality and sensitivity. Give thanks for all that you have learned and experienced together and ask God to help you share the good news you've studied with others in the coming weeks.

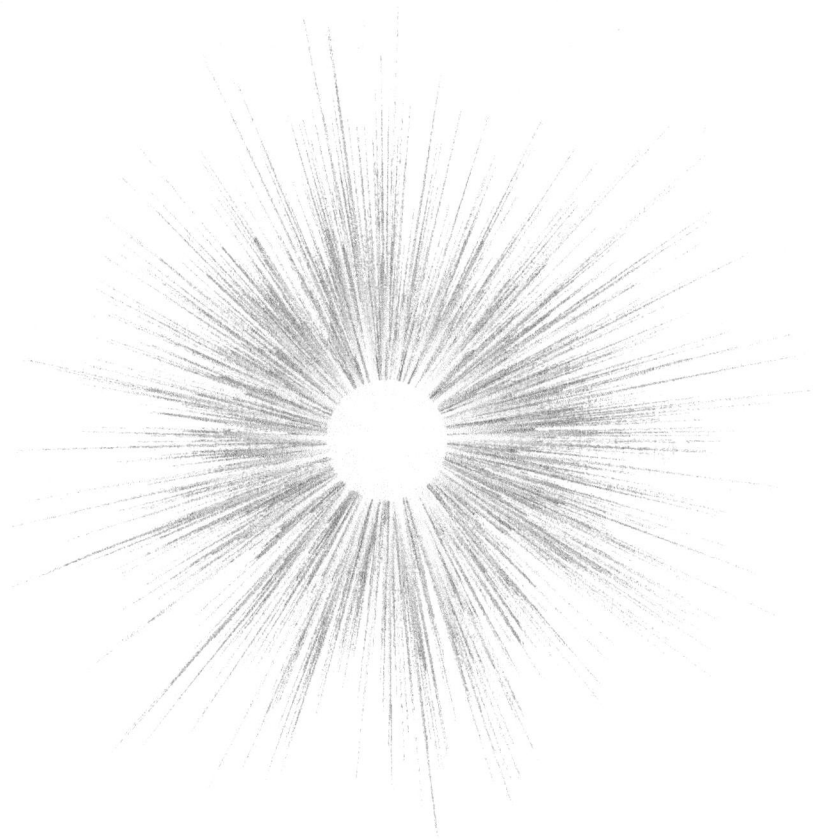

Video Viewer Guide Answers

Introductory Video

physically / spiritually

social media, television, material possessions

prayer, Bible study, worship, journaling, silence

tasks / relationships

telling others the Good News about the wonderful grace of God

birthed / sustains

Week 1

passion for God / God's Power

information / transformation

very presence of God

prayer

fix

action

Week 2

God's Message / mess

mess / age

God's Message / service

God's Message / communicate it clearly

partnership / full ownership

Week 3

law / letter / spirit

Jesus / religion

one thing / another

want / need

push back / freedom steps

Week 4

grace / others / we

disagreements

face, face / listen / ask questions / Scriptures

Exit

Week 5

overwhelming / apathetic

faithfulness

dependency

humility

Week 6

doormat

treat

Disney World

daily / distant

power / message / freedom / grace / mission / direction

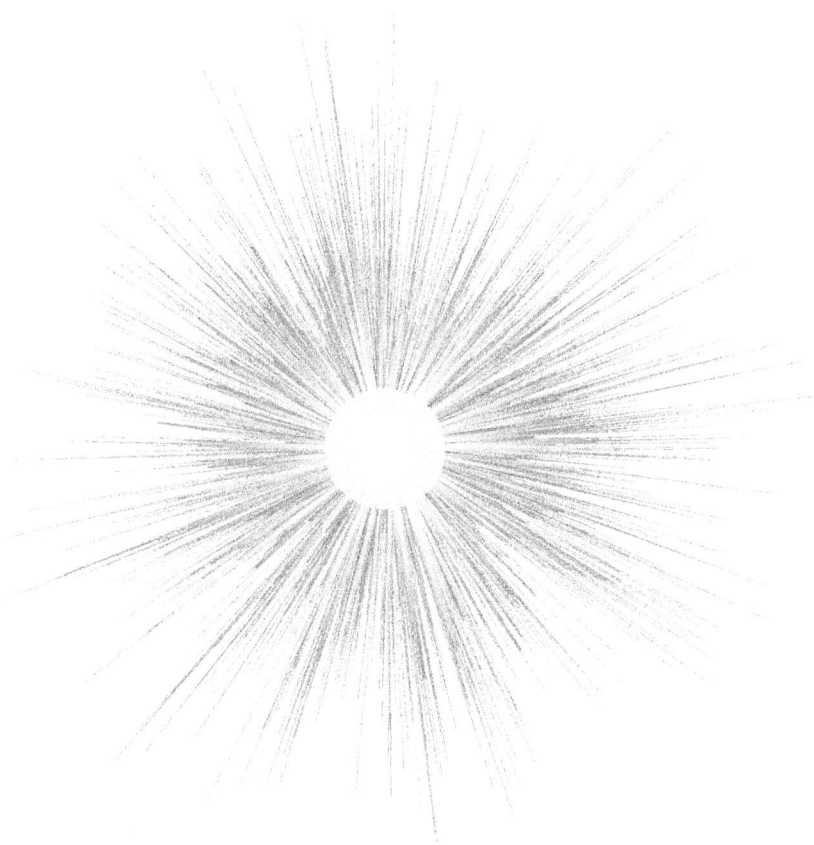

Note

1. Dave Ferguson and Jon Ferguson, *Exponential: How You and Your Friends Can Start a Missional Church Movement* (Grand Rapids, MI: Zondervan, 2010), 58, 63.